Applied Tasseography

A Practical Guide to Interpreting Tea Leaves

by Emily Paper

Applied Divination
Redmond

Published by Applied Divination

ISBN 978-1-7356170-9-1

Book design by Emily Paper

First printing edition 2022

Applied Divination
www.applieddivination.com
info@applieddivination.com

Contents

Introduction

Why tea leaves?

Why *not* tea leaves!?

The ancient art of tasseography - aka tasseomancy or tea leaf reading - ages back countless centuries, to ancient empires and war-torn colonial battles, through to modern day revolutions and directly into your kitchen. Tea plants themselves survive for millennia, and when something has grown, seen, and touched such complex, fascinating history - from well before homo sapiens even walked the earth - how can it not also anticipate and explore our possible futures?

Tasseography is not magic, witchcraft, or woo-woo stuff, although it could certainly be used in any of those practices. Instead, it's a simple way for tea drinkers to find wisdom and guidance from within themselves. When we focus intention and energy into the dregs of our teacup, the leaves act as a mirror to our own intuition.

As a practical and *applied* way to divine the future, tea leaves are a cheap, easy tool for seeing what we can often easily spot in others, but that we often don't see in ourselves.

For example, when I was job hunting and wondering what I could do with my life next, I brewed myself a quick cup of Cubby Wubby Womb Room blend from Adagio Teas[1], and straight-up asked the cup to tell me.

What I first spotted in my cup was a massive Jack Pine, like something out of a Tom Thompson painting, stretching across the immediate future, the mid future, and the far future. The *Plants* section of this book explains that they represent growth, development, and potentially new jobs too. That's great! That's exactly what I wanted to know. Now, to narrow it down even further, we can see that *Trees* represents prosperity (yay!) and *Pine trees* represent peace and contentment. So, whatever I do next in my role will be peaceful. I like that.

---

[1] I don't work for Adagio nor am I sponsored by them; They don't even know I exist, I just love their blends.

It doesn't quite get me to an answer of what I *could* do, however. So, if I keep looking, I spot what looks *to me* like some high-heeled boots in the future. Boots represent travel, leadership, and hard work. I'm not a huge fan of hard work, but now I know what to look for in my next role – travel and leadership. On it!

It's a teacup on a paper plate. I'm not classy. I also admit my Jack Pine could look like a weird gorilla. But that's ambition-friendly, too.

How to brew the leaves and use this book

Think of this book as a reference, not a novel. You do not need to read it front to back, nor should you. This book is for looking up simple shapes you spot in the tea leaves from the bottom of your cup.

Steps:
1. Boil water
2. Stuff an infuser or tea pot with loose leaf tea.
   ! The more haphazard the stuffing, the more tea leaves you may end up with in your cup, so no need to be tidy about it!
3. Let the tea steep
4. Pour yourself a cup
5. Enjoy your nice, hot tea until there are only a few drops - and a lot of leaves - left at the bottom
   ! Don't think you have enough leaves? Add a few from the infuser before you start swirling
6. Swirl the remaining leaves around the bottom of the cup, using a clockwise or counter-clockwise, circular motion (depending on your handed-ness.)

7. If there is too much liquid still in the bottom of
   the cup, place the saucer on top of it, then in one
   swift movement flip it over to get the last dribbles
   out, and turn the cup upright.
8. Note all the blatantly obvious shapes in the cup, and
   where they are positioned.
     ! It may be fuzzy or feel like searching in the
     dark – that's okay! Let your mind adjust. The tea
     plants have been around for centuries, they can
     wait a bit longer for your mind's eye to start
     seeing shapes.
9. Take note of where in the cup the symbols lie, and
   flip to the section on cup layout to interpret the
   timing.
10. This book is alphabetical by category then symbol, so
    first flip to the obvious category, then try the
    direct symbol. If you don't see your item listed, use
    the more general term (for example, if you're sure
    you see a Delorean[2], interpret it based on 'car')
11. Every symbol in this book is followed by *practical
    advice*, which is a task, career, chore, snack, or
    person to reach out for if you need something to do.

What tea do I use?

1. Use loose-leaf tea. Bagged tea is convenient, but you
aren't going to get enough tea leaves falling out of it
to do a valid reading. An exception might be if you rip
the bag open, but is that cheating? I don't know, you
are your own judge here.

2. Do not use herbal tea. Herbal tea is not tea. It's
certainly delicious, but herbal tea is a combination of
dried spices, fruits, bark, and plants that are not tea
plants. Only black, green, white, or oolong teas are
real tea, grown from the tea plants which have lived for
hundreds of years (only the leaves of tea plants are
harvested for teas, the plants remain in place.) Tea
plants have witnessed history; dried fruits have only
been around a few weeks.

3. If you require sugar in your tea, mix it in when you
add the hot water to your leaves. When the leaves have

---

[2] But if you seriously can see a Delorean in your tea leaves,
maybe the 'journey' a car represents is one that takes you back
in time! Amazing insight.

already settled in your cup, too much stirring will alter the results.

4. If your cup doesn't have a lot of tea leaves in it after steeping, feel free to add a few more from the bottom of the tea pot or infuser.

Capture or draw it

Symbols in tea leaves are often hard to place right away, but in our rushed lives we want answers *now*! If you're confused about what you're looking at, snap a pic for analysis later, or doodle the images. Sometimes drawing the shapes makes them "pop" more.

There are blank pages available in this book for you to draw what you see or come up with your own shapes. Better yet, pick up a copy of the *Divination Journal* from Applied Divination[3] and keep detailed notes.

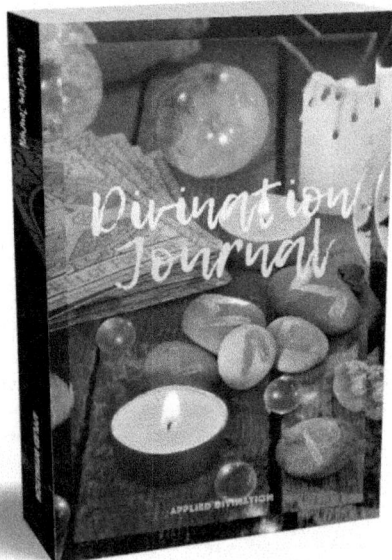

---

[3] Available at https://amzn.to/3ozybl2

The Layout of the Cup

Timing is everything

There are a few ways to read time in your teacup. You can pick and choose a method that works for you, or follow your own timeline. Do whatever is in your heart!

The first is the 12-month, "year ahead" method. The teacup handle represents today, and as we move clockwise around the teacup, each 12th represents a month of the upcoming year. Wherever your shapes fall tells you what to expect during that month.

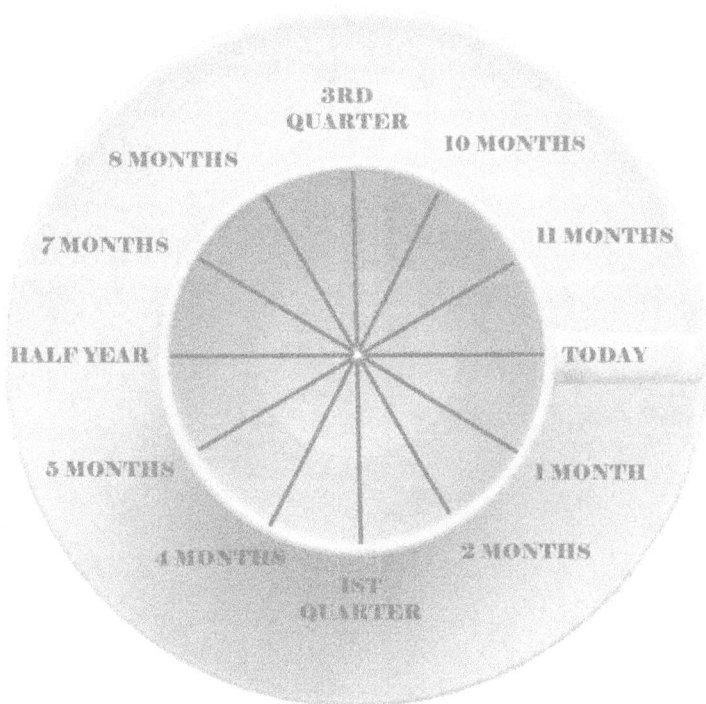

3RD QUARTER

8 MONTHS   10 MONTHS

7 MONTHS   11 MONTHS

HALF YEAR   TODAY

5 MONTHS   1 MONTH

4 MONTHS   2 MONTHS

1ST QUARTER

If you are holding the mug with the handle on the other side, it still counts as today, and you still read the months in a clockwise direction.

An alternate take on the 12-month method is to add a circle in the middle (sometimes the flat part of the teacup, or whatever size you deem fit) and make it the distant future. Then you'll have a reasonable idea as to what is to come sooner *and* later.

I like to use this timing method for younger adults and older children. This is because kids' pasts are usually determined or scripted more by their parents and K-12 education, but their future is almost always wide open.

Note: I don't recommend you read the tea leaves of young children, firstly because they often aren't able to consent to having their fortunes divined, and secondly because *why are you feeding babies caffeine?!*

But whatever, carry on with your bad self.

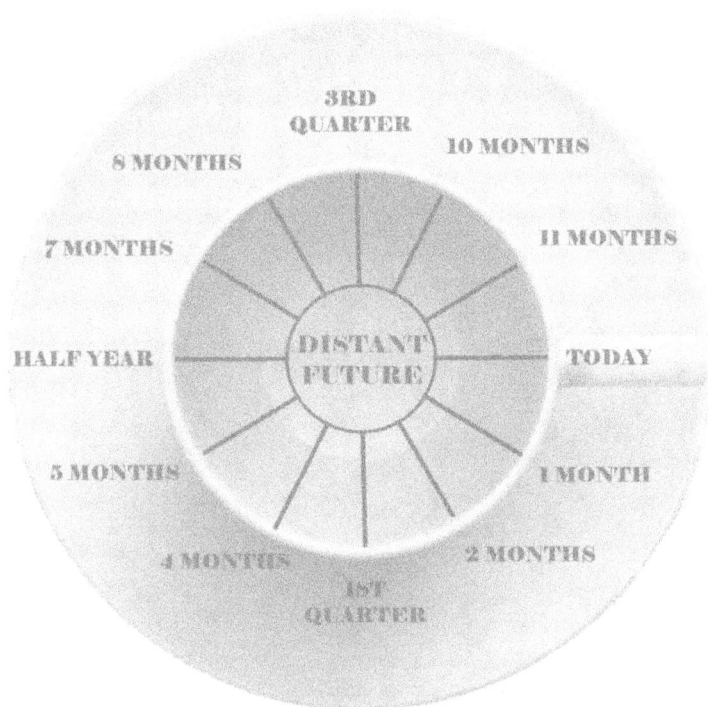

Next is the Past-Present-Future layout. The time still spins clockwise, as in the 12-month method, but now we're not only looking ahead, but we're also looking at what happened in the past to get us where we are now. This gives some insight into how we got where we are.

Some readers flip these dates around, where the future/outcome is near the rim of the cup, and the distant past is at the very bottom. Your choice.

You can see that the area around the handle is still marked "today." Other readers mark it as "the self," meaning anything in there relates to you specifically, or "home" meaning anything in there is about your dwelling and family. I prefer my teacups to be about timing. Maybe I just don't care to know that much about myself!

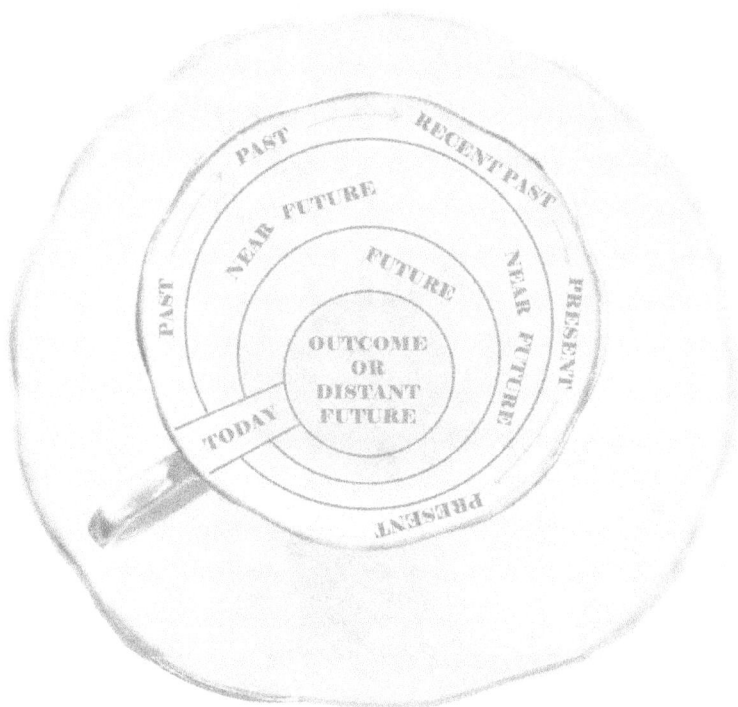

Edwardian fortune-telling cups

Back in the days of King Edward, fortune-telling became a unique way for the common people to earn a living wage and provide hope for their futures. A variety of teacup designs were created which helped tasseographers by providing dates, symbols, and areas on the cup and saucer that reveal specific things - rather than have the reader try to interpret symbols on their own.

These cups are very useful, especially for a novice, and there are a variety available on websites such as Amazon or Etsy. Alternatively, browsing antique shops will sometimes uncover some unique and vintage teacups with shapes which you can interpret in your own way.

I do not own an Edwardian teacup, so I interpret my own symbols, times, and dates in a way that makes sense to me at the time of the reading, but here are some images of possible cups you might encounter in your shopping adventures:

Zodiac Fortune Telling Cups

Also from the wonderful era that was the Edwardian times, we have zodiac or astrological cups.

These are fairly restrictive because they're more about timing and personal zodiac charts than they are about divining day-to-day adventures. However, they're still a neat item to find at a vintage shop, and to drink tea out of, so have at it!

What about this saucer?

Traditional tea leaf readers use the saucer to flip the cup over so they can drain excess fluid. Then they rest their spoons on it and call the saucer's work finished.

This is great, it makes the saucer a useful part of the process, so we can keep our spaces tidy and go on with our reading. I love practicality.

-But I don't love abandoning very useful tea leaves.

When I read, I like to make sure no leaf is wasted, and I read the ones abandoned on the saucer as items, projects, people, or work that is *missing* from my life. I see it as a message about scenarios that perhaps I haven't even considered before, or things and actions I could pursue to make my life complete.

Got some tea leaves on your saucer? Either go ahead and ignore 'em or interpret them as incomplete life lessons or items you're missing out on.

I *leave* no *leaves* behind!

Animals

Like any living creature, animals are interactive. They may represent an action to take, a person who will help or guide you, a gift you will receive, or some aspect of your own personality.

Aardvark – explore negative emotions and work with them
   Dig into negative thoughts | talk to a friend

Albatross – danger at sea
   Read or watch *The Perfect Storm* | eat fish

Alligator – personal disturbances and worry
   Talk to a therapist | clean the closets

Ant – unity, working for the greater good
   Watch *Ghostbusters* | Help out with group projects

Anteater – success after difficulties; sticking to plan
   Mind small obstacles | don't panic | stick to it

Antelope – decisiveness, speed, leap before you look
   Climb a mountain | eat granola

Ape – a malicious and dangerous enemy
   Play a board game | watch fight club

Armadillo – empathy; protection; peace
   Protect yourself | cozy up with a blanket

Axolotl – great health and potential to heal
Be a doctor | heal others | illnesses fade

Badger – a pleasant and successful single life
   Go on a retreat | learn something new | watch *UHF*

Barnacle – a leader speaks his mind; annoyances
      Pay attention | deal with small challenges

Bat – illness; Perhaps death when read with other signs
      Stock the first aid kit | visit a gravesite

Bears

      Bears symbolize strength, courage, protection, nobility, and playfulness

      Travel to the North | watch *The Revenant* | play with children | hibernate (nap)

      Black bear – knowing who you are & what you want
      Brown bear – harmony and integrity
      Grizzly bear – strength; bravery; empowerment
      Koala bear – grounding yourself in the present
      Panda – solitude; protection of the home
      Polar Bear – a trip to a cold climate; blankets

Beaver – creativity, innovation, harmony, cooperation
      Tidy the house | cooperate with peers | paint

Beaver dam – a mysterious space filled with good energy
      Try a new restaurant | take a tour | build a home

Bee – success through your own skills; entrepreneurship
      Visit a school | be confident | smell the flowers

Beehive – Anxiety plus hard work nets positive results
      Focus | ask for help | bake sweet treats

Beetle – domestic problems. Problems in relationships
> **Watch a breakup movie | go be alone | eat tacos**

Birds

> Birds signify emotional experiences or self-development.

> **Join a nonprofit board | take up falconry | visit a school | travel (migrate, like birds!)**

> **Bird Cage** – entrapment, but it may be temporary
> **Bird Nest** –positive omen about good relationships
> **Black Corvids – Crow, Raven, etc** – gloomy news; death; a warning
> **Canary** – workaholic; life force; spiritual
> **Chicken** – new hobbies and interests
> **Cockatoo** – a harmful relationship
> **Dove** – happiness; love; progress toward success
> **Duck** – profitable ventures
> **Eagle** – beneficial changes; inheritance
> **Emu** – a risk-taker
> **Falcon** – fear, or an enemy approaches
> **Flamingo** – seek friends and share emotions
> **Goose** – a difficult visitor; foiled plans
> **Hawk** – an awkward situation
> **Heron** – patience and good luck
> **Hummingbird** – grace; cheerfulness; quick work
> **Jay** – develop your courage and resistance
> **Kingfisher** – a knock at the door brings news
> **Ostrich** – creativity, public upheavals
> **Owl** – misfortune, ominous advice
> **Ox** – quietude; peaceful times ahead
> **Parrot** – international travel, mental energy

Peacock – purchase of new property, fancy dress

Pelican – news from an isolated friend

Penguin – a discovery

Pigeon – news, as a homing pigeon brings

Robin – good fortune

Rooster – a wakeup call, a warning

Seagull – an upcoming storm or news

Stork – fraudulent activities; a baby is coming

Swallow – a most pleasant journey

Swan – separation from loved ones

Vulture – evil or a powerful enemy; sorrow

Woodpecker – pleasant news from the countryside

Fig. 1

On the sides of my morning cuppa, I see a spider, (inheritance), a small heron (patience), and the number 3 (imagination.) In the base I see a garden with wisteria (love,) and maybe a Yucca plant (new job.) Looks great, although I'd rather not inherit (spider) anything right now. I can be patient for that (heron.). Stay alive, fam, I love you (wisteria.) I'll just get a new job (yucca!) I'll think of something (3)!

Bison or Buffalo – an unexpected confusing event; dismay
Stop procrastinating | answer calls | pay bills

Boar or Pig – ambitious but unfocused energy
Write down ideas or plans | sweep the porch

Bull – misfortune
Cancel your plans | fix your car | watch *Rent*

Butterfly – the power of attraction; many admirers
Go on a date | visit Paris | go to a club

Calf – kindness; gentle care with associates
Invite friends over | play volleyball | eat pizza

Camel – travel; endurance; conservation
Visit Africa | go on a tour | clean the car

Caterpillar – someone is being deceptive; gossip
Cancel plans | distrust friends | clean the table

Cats

Cats are devious tricksters. Watch for worries and trouble, especially among family

Change your tactics | Master an illusion | clean the office | eat donuts | watch *Now You See Me*

Cheetah – situations will rapidly evolve
Cougar – secrets
Housecat/domestic – protection; magic
Leopard – strength and agility; rare beauty

Lion – justice; might; authority

Lynx - divorce

Panther – a friendship suffers disloyalty

Snow Leopard – intuition; trust your instincts

Tiger – strength; power; ambition

Chameleon – rapid adaptation to any situation

Learn to juggle | prepare to adapt | dye your hair

Chicken/Hen – bad luck; being used; gossip

Avoid indulgence | don't speak ill | keep secrets

Chipmunk – something delightful is on its way to you

Stay alert | eat nuts | engage life fully

Cobra – terrible danger to you or your family

Clean a bad mess | prepare emergency supplies

Coral – wisdom; longevity

Visit the library | go back to school | dance

Coyote – trickery; adaptability

Change the locks | do banking | watch *Home Alone*

Cow/Cattle – peace and prosperity; a calm mind

Pet the cat | meditate | play music

Crab – disagreements

Get a management job | debate | visit Reno, NV

Crocodile – remain true to your vision and voice

Develop your skills | set goals | make sandwiches

Deer – failure in business ventures
    Quit your job | clean cobwebs and dust

Dingo – revered by Indigenous as creators; exploration
    Make something | paint | write | travel | explore

Dinosaur – persistence; lack of knowledge
    Be flexible | study history | visit a museum

Dogs

Dogs have many meanings which must be interpreted with other symbols. Large dogs are generally protective, small dogs are difficulties.

Watch *The Truman Show* | become a security guard | pay bills | check your security system

Greyhounds and hound dogs – courage and loyalty
Mastiffs and working dogs – an unexpected
        Emergency; an urgent message
Poodle and non-working – seek more information
Retriever or sporting dogs – confidence; trust
        your instincts
Terriers – low self-esteem
Toy dogs – braggadociousness; affluence

Donkey – untapped potential
    Enroll in school | take challenges | carry boxes

Dragonfly – adaptation and transformation
    Reinvent yourself | eat outside | watch the MCU

Earwig - transformation outside and in

Tour the tropics | light a fire | clean your ears

Eel - discovering friends are enemies

Watch The Princess Bride | eat sushi | distrust

Elephant - power; travel; friendship

Plan trips | call pals | watch your step | recycle

Elk - inner strength; dignity; power

Stay on course | see things through | head north

Ferret - earth; diplomacy

Be friendly | ask questions | recycle

Firefly - inner light; mystery and magic

Nurture others so they find their inner light

Fish

Because fish are only in the water, they generally represent news or items from overseas. (yes, I am aware whales & dolphins aren't fish.)

Check the mail | visit a foreign land | go swimming | change jobs | read a new genre

Betta - prosperity; fertility; housewarming gift
Dolphin - emotions and intellect, guidance
Fish (unidentified) - good health; announcement
Jellyfish - flow, instinct, movement
Oysters - a luxurious lifestyle

Salmon – news of fortune and prosperity

Shrimp/Prawns – a satisfactory resolution

Seahorse – good luck, power

Shark – death, money trouble

Starfish – luck

Stingray – may different paths ahead

Whale – be cautious

Urchin – fertility; femininity

Fly – irritations

Clean windows | eat fast food | watch *Booksmart*

Fox – theft; disloyalty

Go to court | right a wrong | apologize | forgive

Frog – a life change, such as new residence or new job

Jump rope | start a business | join a protest

Gorilla – prominence in career; achievement of ambition

Create a trophy shelf | celebrate | eat a cake

Giraffe – misinformation spreads

Tell the truth | solve a puzzle | watch *Idiocracy*

Goat – a risky new venture; danger

Fix a hazard | clear clutter | paint with orange

Hamster – adventure; health; energy; joy

Run a marathon | dine with family | create

Hedgehog – a surprise engagement

Bake pie | surprise someone | try something new

Hippopotamus – health and fertility; calmness
  Tend to the garden | eat watermelon | call mom

Horse – loyal friends; happiness; changes
  Call friends | dine out | eat chips and dip

Insects – unidentified: small issues are easily overcome
  Clear clutter | deal with bugs | feed the birds

Jackal – desolation; destruction
  Reach out to people | buy a
  fire extinguisher

Kangaroo – interesting news
  List your goals | check the mail | read the news

Lamb – a risky business proves successful
  Sweep the front hall | watch *The Game* | invest |
  try something new

Lemur – spirit of the ancestors; good luck
  Thank your elders | invite ancestors to dinner

Lizard – deceit; a liar
  Be skeptical | call recruiters | use green

Lobster – a gift
  Give gifts | go fishing | help someone | do art

Mice – poverty; loss
  See the doctor | watch *Les Mis* | apply for grants

Mole – enemies in the midst

> Beware others | set mouse traps | ignore doorbell

Monkey – rumors; grief

> Have a cry | listen for gossip about yourself

Moose – elegance; attraction; individuality

> Get a haircut | lose weights | have courage

Moth – rebirth; resurrection; regeneration; moon energy

> Trust your inner wisdom | visit a psychic

Mythical Creatures

> Mythical beings imply fantasy or magic. They could signify dreams or nightmares coming true.
>
> Learn a magic trick | read a fantasy novel | visit ancient sites | eat superfoods | watch *LOTR*
>
> **Angel** – protection; being watched over
> **Cerberus** – death; the underworld; guarding
> **Dragon** – sudden and dangerous changes
> **Demon/Devil** – distress; fear; annoyances
> **Elf** – magical nature; beautiful sunset
> **Fairy** – something magical happens soon
> **Gnome or Leprechaun** – good luck; hidden treasure
> **Griffin/Gryphon** – courage and boldness needed
> **Hydra** – male struggles
> **Mermaid** – female power; mother nature; danger at sea; changing weather
> **Sasquatch** – separating fact from fiction; hiding
> **Sphinx** – your hopes are too large, think smaller

Unicorn – a scandalous event

Werewolf – untamed energy; primal urges

Troll – destructive instincts; a menace

Octopus – a warning

Do the right thing | fix fire alarms | take care

Otter – friends may be scheming behind your back; shock

Be wary of friends | watch the news | eat popcorn

Ox – hospitality

Take a bath | visit a spa | travel to the coast

Pig – success in agriculture; the gift of wealth; greed

Plant seeds | adopt a plant | give gifts

Porcupine – children; questions; crossroads

Decide | watch *Sliding Doors* | accept truth

Rabbit – friends return; a journey; news about a child

Visit a baby | watch *Waitress* | adopt a bunny

Raccoon – deception; scavenging

Feed animals | wear a mask | go dumpster diving |
play silly pranks

Rat – troubles

Prepare for disappointment | do taxes | snack

Ram – upcoming difficulties

Slow down | visit Los Angeles | buy a car

Rhinoceros – a risky undertaking

      Tour a museum | watch Jurassic Park | take a risk

Scorpion – pride; passion

      Brag a little | join a nonprofit | donate money

Seal – hard work will lead to success

      Be an environmentalist | watch *Wall-E* | drink tea

Shark – death; sudden and unexpected change

      Attend a funeral | visit a grave | prepare

Sheep – an omen of success and prosperity

      Write your will | eat fruits | watch *Anastasia*

Skunk – fear; warning; danger

      Stay alert | watch *Loony Tunes* | be careful

Sloth – relaxation; conserving energy; groundedness

      Be at peace | take naps | chill out | climb trees

Slug – small bothersome things

      Refill mousetraps or bug catchers | clear |
      debug software

Snail – mischief; infidelity

      Beware cheaters | go to a dive bar | drink beer

Snake/reptiles – danger; misfortune; illness

      See a doctor | watch a horror film | walk dogs

Spider – inheritance

> Pass down family recipes | call family | be happy

Squirrel – cheerfulness; ADHD

> Meditate | decorate shiny things | watch sunsets

Swan – a happy love life; monogamy

> Get married | date | watch *The Princess Bride*

Toad – be careful; malicious intent

> Watch your back| visit Las Vegas

Tortoise – misrepresentation

> Stop lying | visit a park | go canoeing

Turtle – steady progress toward luxury; wealth

> Set big goals | invest in a retirement plan

Turkey – you make a dangerous mistake

> Prepare emergency supplies | sharpen knives

Walrus – family ties; friendship

> Call family | reach out to friends | give hugs | visit an aquarium

Wasp – problems in a relationship

> Sort email inbox | get divorced | do your nails

Weasel – someone is trying to trick you

> Set up a security system | watch your back

Whale – use caution, danger is afoot
   Buy boots | use a flashlight | watch *Ant-Man*

Wolf – protection is needed; keep defenses up
   Build a fence | visit battlegrounds | eat noodles

Worm – evil; misfortune
   Drink wine | visit the casino | the answer is no

Zebra – foreign policy; anticipated event is a letdown
   Go to zoo | don't get hopes up | visit Toronto

Notes, doodles, or other animals you see:

Fig. 2

Our youngest son, Jack, sees a small dove at the
5-month mark, a large dragon above a camel at the
6-month mark, and some dots and dashes for the
rest of the year.

So, he should be happy and make progress (dove),
but then a sudden and dangerous change might
happen during travel (dragon and camel - oh no!)
Later this year he'll be working hard and making
money (dots and dashes - sweet, that's what a Mom
likes to see!)

Plants

Plants represent growth and development. Depending on how significant the plant is in your cup, it could represent a life-changing development (such as the birth of a child), a new job, or it could represent a smaller aspect of your life such as your daily wellness, residence, or business.

Acorn – something small will have huge effects
Clear clutter | do the laundry | eat dumplings

Anemone – an event in autumn; Look to other symbols
Read *Emma* | give gifts | sell something | garden

Bamboo – Good luck; happy new year; facing adversity
Count your blessings | decorate your home

Belladonna/nightshade – falsehoods; warning; death
Beware bad advice | watch *Robin Hood*

Branch – large: success; broken: failure
Celebrate small wins | visit a woman-owned store

Bush – Bad instincts; A misuse of power or a bad romance
Quit | visit a theme park | read thrillers

Cactus – protection; warmth; motherly love
Call your mom | cuddle under a blanket | stay in

Clover – very good luck; prosperity and success
Welcome good fortune | share the wealth | donate

Eucalyptus – the division of the underworld
Clear your space of negativity | get fresh air

Fern – protection is needed in love or safety
Buy a safer car | people watch | call a handyman

Flowers

Single, unidentified flowers represent new beginnings and favors granted. A **bouquet** of many flowers represents a bounty of friends, love, or money. Also check the flowers in the bouquet.

Start new ventures | smell the roses | redecorate | join a startup | work with animals | eat salad

Baby's breath - everlasting love; innocence

Bird of Paradise - difficulties will soon end

Bluebell - an event will take place next spring. Look to other symbols for clarification

Carnation - friendship and cheer

Daffodil - A wish will come true

Dahlia - an important event in the fall

Daisy - Childhood or children will prove important

Dandelion - an unexpected party invitation

Forget-Me-Not - wishes come true

Hyacinth - commitment; power; The Sun God, Apollo

Iris, Crocus - partnership, together forever

Lilac - Radiance and beauty, happiness

Lily (all) - pregnancy, love and marriage, family

Orchid - Fortune is coming

Pansy - modesty, calm

Peony - an important decision made in the summer

Poppy - a pleasant event in the early summer

Rose - popularity, passion, love

Sunflower - education, study a personal interest

Tulip - good health; long friendships

Violet - lofty ideals; coming joy

Garden – a time of hard work followed by abundance
      Sacrifice now for reward later | clean the fridge

Garland – a joyous event; togetherness; love
      Throw a party | buy a loveseat | go out to eat

Grass – futile attempts to force happiness upon oneself
      Show gratitude | eat a TV dinner | do plumbing

Heather – good luck is around the corner
      Be patient | visit a psychic | follow your dreams

Hedge – Perseverance gets you through difficult times
      Become a teacher | try boxing | watch *Ratatouille*

Holly – Something significant will occur in wintertime
      have holiday party | bake fruitcake | trim trees

Ivy – Patience; loyalty
      Join a nonprofit | eat comfort food | listen

Jade – good luck; positive chi energy
      Call friends | watch *Big Hero 6* or *Finding Nemo*

Laurel wreath – good health and strong bones
      Buy a hammock | stretch | decorate for holidays

Leaves – Prosperity
      Invest | plant seeds | visit with a friend
      Leaves, pile - travel

Lilac – a lasting joy
> Give thanks | eat chocolate | pick flowers

Logs – successful affairs
> Start a project | light a fire | chop wood

Mistletoe – a dream will come true after a long wait
> Write down your dreams | kiss your lover

Mushroom – Lovers separate; gossip; scandal
> Go to the bar | eat Cheetos | clean the bathroom

Nettles – deceit; thievery; mischief
> Check your accounts | watch *Home Alone*

Philodendron – health and abundance; artist's muse
> Draw | eat healthy food | get out in nature

Seaweed – happy memories
> Play with a child | eat your favorite food

Shamrock – good luck and fortune
> Buy a lottery ticket | take a risk | eat cookies

Straw –success in business or industry fortune
> Start a company | change jobs | share your ideas

Tea Tree – sacred rebirth; childbirthing; wellness
> Use tea tree oil | bathe | nourish the soul | Have
> another cup of tea

Timber – successful affairs; good health and well being
Start a project | light a fire | chop wood

Toadstool – Lovers separate; gossip; scandal
Go to the bar | eat Cheetos | clean the bathroom

Topiary – Joyful gifts after a long wait
Check the mail | get together with friends

Trees

Trees generally foretell of health and prosperity. However, a **forest** might be a sign of confusion or feeling lost. What tree is the forest comprised of?

Visit the doctor | take a nap | get a job in healthcare | eat salad | visit the forest

Apple or fruit tree – happiness, health, and
fortune
Branch – large: independence; Broken: failure
Chestnut tree – an important event in the Spring
Christmas tree – the holidays bring unexpected
joy
Elm – prosperity
Evergreens – coziness, comfort
Joshua – an enduring legacy
Magnolia – peace after a difficult period
Maple – intelligence; longevity; generosity
May/Maypole/Hawthorn – the arrival of good news
Oak – strength and wellness, prosperity
Palm – winning a competition, fame

Pine – peace, contentment

Willow tree – fertility and new life

Yew – Legacy, inheritance

Venus Flytrap – persistence; trying again

Trust instincts | watch *Little Shop of Horrors*

Wheat – bounty; resurrection

Farm | bake bread | celebrate your blessings

Wisteria – romance; devotion

Go on a date | spend time with your love

Wood, general – a fortunate event

Light a candle | be creative | eat fruits

Wreath, laurel or headpiece – power; dignity

Ask an expert | lead your team | eat steak

Wreath, display – a symbol of marriage

Become an officiant | get married | bake cake

Yucca – new opportunities; new job

Recycle | the answer is yes | save
the environment

Fig. 3

Our eldest child, Margaret, is studying abroad, and she sent this pic of the leaves remaining from her afternoon tea.

She sees one mighty oak tree under stars in the sky. Oaks signify strength, wellness, and prosperity, and stars bring good luck! The tree takes up much of the cup, so I would say this covers her entire year and more. We always tell her, "Everything is coming up Margaret," and judging by this reading that refrain seems to hold true.

Notes, doodles, or other plants you see:

Food & Food Service

In ancient times, possessing a variety of foods
was a symbol of status, wealth, and power. It is
also an excuse for humans to come together.
Seeing food items in your teacup therefore
represents abundance and relationships.

Note: I only expect tea leaves in your teacup. If
you have *actual* food items in there, you've
brewed something wrong.

Almonds – good luck after a short struggle
Push through the difficulty | eat tomatoes | red

Bacon – a profitable business
Lead | research | drink coffee |
watch *Knives Out*

Basket – a gift from a new friend
Give or receive gifts | buy plants | visit Norway

Beans – financial distress; an argument
Eat pineapple on pizza | choose | sell something

Biscuit – a favorable, joyful event
Work with children | watch *Elf* | play

Bone – gossip; be wary of harm
Cancel plans | watch *Crazy Rich Asians*

Bottle – alcoholism; overindulgence
Quit drinking; have a smoothie; sweep the floor

Bread – Time to seek dietary advice; nutrition
Eat healthy | workout | travel | eat a sandwich

Cabbage – complications at work or with coworkers
Have a meeting | steal your coworker's lunch

Cake – Domestic bliss; festivals
Throw a party | visit community centers | eat cake

Candy – temptation and reward

      Visit Switzerland | read *Of Mice and Men*

Carafe – finding your own pleasure or satisfaction

      Go back to school | persevere | dream big

Cauldron – new job prospects

      Job hunt | ask for a raise | become your own boss

Cauliflower – you are unreliable

      Go shopping | resist laziness | cauliflower pizza

Celery – staying young; exercise

      Run | eat ants on a log | visit the gym

Cereal – harvest

      Plant seeds | buy cereal |

      quit a vice

Champagne – good fortune and prosperous friends

      Count blessings | throw a party | drink champagne

Cheese – richness; luxury; fame

      Watch your fat intake | eat rich foods

Chestnuts – sticking to the plan

      Create a goal and stick to it | complete to-dos

Chicken/turkey (as food) – compromise; work on character

      Accept your mistakes | agree with others

Cucumber – everything goes to plan

      Keep your eyes on the prize | eat salad

Cup – Ignore criticism for your successful projects

      Start a journal | find supporters | eat ice cream

Cocktail – being a loner; isolation; boredom

      Go out with friends | show up | be present

Coffee – strange comforts; dependence

      Visit a farm | plant seeds | break free

Coffeepot – a warning of impending illness

      Prepare emergency supplies | buy band aids

Cork or corkscrew – adaptation

      Move furniture | change something | eat sushi

Corn – Commercial success

      Invest in your business | buy stocks | save money

Cornucopia – great success in all your undertakings

      Eat squash | start a project | weave a basket

Dish – a spat or disagreement

      Back up your data | arm yourself with knowledge

Donut – good times; stereotypes

      Eat a donut | Get into law enforcement | take
      a shower

Dumpling – wealth; gold

>   Celebrate abundance | secure gold jewelry

Egg – Auspicious fortune

>   Feed the chickens | eat a sandwich | count money

Fish (as food) – great fortune

>   Show gratitude | pay bills | find new work

Fruit

>   Fruits generally foretell of prosperity.

>   Treat yourself | share the wealth | throw a party | pick fruits | eat at a fine dining establishment

Apple – achievement and success

Banana – material goods are easy to obtain

Berries – perfection; sweetness in character

Coconut – a tropical vacation

Cherries – a whimsical love affair

Dates – an unexpected joyful event

Fig – abundance and success

Grapes – happiness

Mango – happiness; culture

Melon – your hero shares good information

Orange/Citrus – sunshine; joy; fascination

Pear – comfort and financial peace

Pineapple – a rich friend gives a gift

Stone Fruit (peaches, nectarines, plums, etc) – new ideas; something in development

Strawberries – pleasure and satisfaction

Fork – someone is out to harm you
Learn karate | watch your back | buy forks

Glass dishware – staying true to your values
Do nonprofit work | invest in yourself | eat fish

Glasses, drinking – a party; entertaining friends
Invite over guests | buy wine | smile | toast

Honey – delightful events; prosperity
Throw a party | call friends | bake cakes

Ice – danger
Protect your surroundings | wear boots | shovel

Ice Cream Cone – adaptability; fortitude
Complete tasks | practice work/life balance

Jam or jelly – wasted resources
Check your accounts | throw out the trash | eat

Jug – recognition for important work
Celebrate achievements | get a trophy | eat cake

Keg – a picnic; prosperous times
Have a picnic | share the bounty with others

Kettle – someone who is ill comes to visit
Wear a mask | get vaccinated | prepare hot tea

Knife – fights; broken relationships; wounds
      Sharpen your knives | clean your wounds
      (metaphorically or literally)

Ladle – good health and nourishment; overcoming a cold
      Prepare soup | take vitamins | plan your meals

Leek – a need to uncover the truth
      Do some detective work | eat leek & potato soup

Lettuce – anxiety; nightmares
      Take a Xanax | meditate | write down your dreams

Macaroni – working extra hard just to pay small bills
      Find a second job | analyze your budget

Meat – financial strain; money woes
      Check the couch cushions | find a better job

Mushroom – a relocation out into the country or forest
      Move | clean the storage closets | eat risotto

Mug – a meeting with someone who brings joy
      Get together for coffee | play | paint

Nuts – a time of difficulty passes
      Celebrate | bake a cake | eat fruitcake
      Nutcracker – working hard will be rewarding

Oil and vinegar – blessings; desire toward an opposite
      Go on a date | eat a salad | watch a rom-com

Onion – your secrets revealed by a trusted friend
>Don't divulge information | check the locks

Oyster – the acquisition of wealth
>Count your blessings | check the stock market

Pan – peace in the home
>Stay inside | play an
>instrument | cook

Parsley – satisfaction
>Bake bread | visit Italy | go to an art gallery

Pasta – tradition; timelessness
>Meet friends | eat lasagna | read *Eat, Pray, Love*

Pepper – a difficult secret to keep
>Don't share gossip | have drinks with a friend

Pitcher – boredom
>Read a book | watch TV | watch the big game

Pizza – this has no divine meaning, it's just great food
>Share a pizza with friends | try new toppings

Plate – everything goes to plan
>Invite guests to dinner | celebrate a birthday

Pot – a service to society or a nonprofit
>Join a nonprofit | donate | adopt a pet

Potato – small things are bothersome
　　　Do pest control | light citronella candles

Rice – harmony; inner purity
　　　Stay true to your values |
　　　eat Asian food

Sausage – an illness
　　　Stockpile band aids and vitamins | drink juice

Shrimp/Prawns – arrangements are satisfactory
　　　Make plans | order shrimp | have a cocktail

Sink – feelings turned off and on again
　　　Calm your emotions | wash dishes | journal ideas

Spoon – generous gifts
　　　Give and receive presents | plant garden seeds

Stove – difficulties await you
　　　Prepare paperwork | be mindful of others | cook

Teacup/tea – small things bring great joy
　　　Spend time with a baby or small pets | drink tea

Table – a social event
　　　Get together with friends | call your parents

Tomatoes – fortune increases; a collection grows
　　　Clean the trophy shelf | visit an antique shop

Turnip – an argument with a spouse; cheating

Be wary of your partner | ask questions

Vegetables (general) – hard work followed by rest

Rest after a long day | buy sheets | eat veggies

Wedding cake – a successful and long marriage

Celebrate | get married | buy a new suit or dress

Wine glass – joy and accomplishment

Toast to good health | throw a party | dance

Wishbone – a wish granted

Make a wish

Yogurt – happy news from abroad

Call a friend | change something about yourself

Yorkshire Pudding – slowly moving out of poverty

Dine with friends | look ahead to the future

Fig. 4

I had a late-night tea and hubs noticed this fig. Figs foretell of abundance and success, which I'll gladly take. It appears to also have a few leaves attached to it, which is another sign of prosperity. I had a job interview the next day which seemed to go well, so I'm feeling quite positive!

Notes, doodles, or other food you see:

Objects

Inanimate objects are made by humans, so rather than have a developmental or nurturing meaning, they often represent the day-to-day stuff, such as activities, emotions, or yes/no answers to everyday questions.

Airplane – toward or away: incoming or outgoing news
Receive news | send news | read/watch the news

Alien – eyes on the prize; minor problems
Watch a sci-fi movie | plan your future

Ambulance – good health; illness
Look to other symbols for more information

Anchor – stability in love and friendship; safety
Trust your friends | dine out | go sailing

Angel – good news about relationships
Attend church | meditate | listen

Anvil – strength
Lift weights | carry heavy
boxes | move furniture

Apron – an opportunity to make new friends or contacts
Answer the phone | network | bake

Ark – security in times of distress
Call a friend | check the locks | buy an umbrella

Arrow – bad news from the direction the arrow points
Prepare for bad news | watch the weather

Axe – mastery and skill; Sometimes a relationship *split*
Chop wood | analyze your relationship | study

Award/Medal – you will be rewarded for previous work
Celebrate accomplishments | toast | eat dinner

Bag/Sack – an intriguing event you weren't expecting; items that are important to you arrive
Buy a new suit/dress | clean your closet | go out

Bagpipes – warning; sadness
Attend a funeral | rest | eat hors d'oeuvres

Ball – chance; the night sky
Watch the sunset | make a plan | go camping

Ball & Chain – imprisoned by your own thoughts; unhappy
Face challenges head on | let go of something

Balloon – a passing fancy or new idea, not serious
Write down your ideas but do not engage in them | write a book

Banner – marriage; a wedding
Open the mail | accept an invitation | propose

Baseball Bat – situations require diligence
Take advice from higher-ups | be confident

Basket – satisfaction, happiness
Pick flowers | decorate | care for a pet or baby

Bath – grief; longing; distress
Cry | take baths | visit spas | watch *Pretty Woman*

Bayonet – wounds; a fight

      Prepare for a battle | plant aloe vera

Bed – illness or death; a visit from an old friend

      Lie down | visit sick friends | visit a graveyard

Bell – wonderful news; many bells represents a wedding

      Attend an event | drink champagne | celebrate

Bench – relief; rest

      Sit | sleep | Sit in the park | meditate

Bible – a decision from an authority figure

      Dress well | prepare for hard news | go to church

Bicycle – promising times ahead

      Look forward | take a necessary but hard journey

Billiards/Pool table – listen to others; regret

      Accept advice from friends | listen, don't speak

Boat – success in a new venture; a visiting friend

      Prepare a business plan | clean the garage | sail

Body Parts

Parts of the body tend to be about feelings, thought, and physical health.

Exercise | talk it out | eat healthy food

Arm – love, hugs, strength

Baby – worries, stress, financial trouble

Breasts – nourishment; childhood

Child – new projects

Ear – shocking news

Eye – solving difficult problems

Face – many: an invitation, one: rudeness

Finger – adjoining symbols need attention

Fist – Anger, fights

Foot – you must make a decisive move

Hair – physical strength; virility; seduction

Hand – a sign of partnership, a meeting

Head – family trouble, mental distress

Heart – the arrival of joy, satisfaction

Human – a visitor arrives

Knee – reach out to an advisor; planning

Leg – fortunate events

Nose – a changed mind; a wayward idea

Skeleton – disturbing information; judging others

Skull – concentration; connection with divinity

Teeth – go to the dentist; sadness

Thumb – an opportunity to impress others

Tongue – running at the mouth; bad words

Bomb – radical change; personal disaster; loss of life
Be careful with fireworks | buy an extinguisher

Bone – misfortune
Check your accounts | chat with family

Book – a desire to learn something brand new
Read | go to a bookstore | write | study

Boomerang – Australia, perhaps travel or news therein
Visit Australia | contact an Australian friend

Boot – success in business; higher income
Start a new job | start your business | buy boots

Bow & Arrow – your personal secrets are revealed
Try archery | eat popcorn | keep a low profile

Box – open: secrets revealed; Closed: found objects
Gossip with friends | receive or give a package

Bracelet – a discovery
Travel somewhere new | weave | invest in gemstones

Bridge – lucrative travel plans; an opportunity
Plan a trip | say yes | fix the car | drink juice

Broom – don't open up too soon; untrustworthy friends
Stay quiet | sweep the floors | don't answer calls

Bubble – a roller-coaster of emotions
Blow bubbles | talk it out | visit a park

Building – corporate greed; eviction
Pay your landlord | quit your
job | go downtown

Buoy – the ability to withstand all weather; friends
Buy a coat | go sailing with friends | go fishing

Bus – a need to share your ideas with others

> Write a letter | film a TikTok | share ideas

Buttons – suggestions which are never practiced

> Listen to advice | your advice won't be heeded

Cabinet – an unexpected discovery

> Look through old items | clean out cabinets

Camera – clever new ideas

> Take up photography | write down your plans

Camp/Camping – difficult relationships; a menace

> Get together with friends | mind your stuff

Candle – trials and tribulations; illness

> Manage emergency supplies | pray | visit church

Cannon – military or naval success

> Light fireworks | thank a service person

Canoe – friends to lovers

> Go on a canoe trip | download a dating app

Car – short visits with friends; good luck

> Go for a drive | plant shamrocks | celebrate

Cards

> It is said that each suit represents one of the four pillars of the Middle Ages. Hearts – the Church, Spades – the military, Diamonds – the merchant class, Clubs – agriculture.

If you spot a specific, numbered card, look to the "Letters and Numbers" section for more info.

Clubs – news
Diamonds – an incoming sum of money
Hearts – affection and happiness in your home
Spades – buildings; a city; architecture

Carriage – creature comforts; Without a horse: loss
Ride a rickshaw | visit a graveyard or park

Castle – fortune; If old/broken: disappointment
Visit a kingdom | clean windows | call a friend

Cave – remaining hidden; obscurity
Read a mystery | go hiking | solve a problem

Chain – a dilemma; a wedding
Accept invitations | make a bracelet | knit

Chair – a guest arrives
Answer the door | throw a party | sit

Chimney – a common life; with smoke: comfort
Light a fire | be bored | read a book

Church – legacy
Write your will | go to church

Cigar – a wealthy friend steals your ideas
Protect your assets | don't share ideas

Cloak/Cape – a shield; a feeling of invincibility
        Be careful | think on your feet | solve mysteries

Clock – a desire to rush through the present
        Check time | slow down | remember what you forgot

Cloud – failure; sadness
        Check the weather | mope around | cloudgaze

Clown – everyone laughs at you; fear
        Work through your anxiety | buy shoes | be a clown

Coal – prosperity
        Light a fire | invest your assets | have a BBQ

Coat – sadness at a split or divorce
        help a friend going through a breakup | buy coats

Coffin – a bad omen; death
        Look to other symbols for timeline or more info

Coin or coins – monetary wealth; motherhood
        Take control of finances | have a baby

Comb – trust in others is compromised
        Be wary of con artists | comb your hair

Comet – an unusual turn of events. Good weather
        Roll the dice | take a chance | go outside

Compass – travel for work

    Plan a trip | go hiking | take on a new project

Cork – buoyancy of spirit; lightheartedness

    Work on new business | drink wine | be responsible

Crown – the attainment of highest honor; advancement

    Give gifts | show gratitude | celebrate

Crutches – upcoming illness

    Watch your step | fix broken items | buy crutches

Curtain – something will be revealed; secrets

    Spy on the neighbors | contact a friend

Dagger – ominous sign; danger

    Secure your valuables | stay in | watch out

Dance or Dancer – pleasant news arrives

    Check messages | go dancing | watch a dance show

Dart – a struggle; intense anger

    Remain calm | take a chill pill | stay inside

Dead body/Death – a need for inner growth; expansion

    Visit a career coach | get out of your comfort zone | renovate your home or office

Desk – correspondence of bad news

    Tidy an office | mentally prepare | eat trail mix

Doll – apathy

      Take a nap | dust the tchotchkes | watch TV

Dress – protection; hidden desires; secrets

      Wear a dress | go to a secret place | play poker

Drums – a dangerous journey ahead

      Clean out your bags | do laundry | listen to rock

Dumbbell – meeting new people

      Go to the gym | get a haircut | watch *Forrest Gump*

Dustpan – happiness is around the corner

      Stay upbeat | sweep the floor | comfort a friend

Earring – elegance; control

      Update your wardrobe | strut | be strong

Easel – goods; marriage; children

      Make creative art | get married | go shopping

Engine – journeys; news

      Fix your car | travel abroad | find new work

Envelope – finding money; an introvert

      Keep your eyes open | sit quietly with friends

Extinguisher – a difficult event

      Replace your fire extinguisher | prepare supplies

Fig. 5

In my husband's cup I see darts (anger, struggle),
a screw (hard work) and a ladder (helpful leader.)

Reading from past through future, it shows intense
frustration (this happens to him a lot at work,)
perseverance (he also works very hard, though) and
a future where an influential leader helps him
gain fortune. Not too shabby!

Explosion – a fresh start; hard truths; upset friends

   Be honest, but tactful | try something new

Eyeglasses – a discovery; a surprise

   Visit the eye doctor | answer calls | eat carrots

Fan – being admired; romance
> Download a dating app | go on a date

Feathers – achievement; literary success; change
> Write a book | go bird watching | switch jobs

Fence – something is blocking your success
> Go over your plans | consult an expert

Fire – destruction; passion; illumination
> Burn things | watch *True Romance* | light a candle

Flag – rebellion; war; danger
> Play a competitive sport | start an argument

Football – outdoor play
> Visit the park | play sports | go to a splash pad

Fountain – happiness; prosperity; legacy
> Invest | write a will | get together with family

Garter – dislike of a woman
> Watch for an unlikeable woman | call your mom

Gate – an opportunity awaits
> Accept invitations | answer calls | fix the gate

Giant – confrontation; a friend is actually an enemy
> Fight | show courage | be prepared

Golf clubs – a workaholic; no play
   Analyze work/life balance | go golfing

Grave – generally a message of sorrow; despair
   Look to other symbols for timeline or more info

Guard – the weak are protected; control negativity
   Be positive | change your lifestyle | stay safe

Guitar – an attraction; an affair
   Play or write music | go on a date | start a band

Gun – sudden destruction; violence
   Be careful | lockup weapons | secure the fortress

Hammer – annoying chores that must be done
   Do the annoying chores | build things

Hammock – something you looked forward to isn't fun
   Lower your expectations | hang out in a hammock

Handbell – a desire to please your friends
   Have a get-together | cater an event | play ball

Handcuffs – imprisonment; misfortune
   Don't speed | be wary of your actions | be good

Harp/Lyre – sadness; a mental illness
   Speak to a therapist | go to a concert

Hat – a friend arrives; successful ventures
>>> Answer the door | launch a business | set goals
>>> **Helmet** – conflict with that friend

Hill – overcoming challenges; resilience
>>> Don't look back | go for a hike | eat a picnic

Hockey Stick or Puck – gaming skill
>>> Practice | play competitive sports | see a game

Hoop – expended energy on unimportant tasks; joy
>>> Play | go dancing | run a marathon | have fun

Horns – a foe nears
>>> Be wary of others | don't answer the door

Horseshoe – wishes come true
>>> Make a wish | go horseback riding | play lottery

Hourglass – a delay in plans
>>> Patience | don't count chickens before they hatch

House – a new home; a successful event
>>> Go **house hunting** | have a **get-together** |
>>> **redecorate** your room or house

Initials – these point to names of people or items
>>> See the Letters & Numbers section for more info

Ink/Ink pot – communication; creativity; permanence
>>> Look for inspiration | draw | become a writer

Iron – small chores will irritate you, but pass quickly
     Do the laundry | clean up | declutter

Ivory – industry; wealth through ill-gotten gains
     Lead with integrity | save the elephants

Javelin – dominance; strength; masculinity
     Protect others | lift weights | join a fun game

Jewelry – presents; an increase in wealth
     Give and receive gifts | check bank balances

Joker/Jester – silly things; ignoring important work
     Read a joke book | go to a comedy show | behave

Jumping – advantageous events
     Accept invitations | buy a new suit or dress

Key – situations will improve; success is at hand
     Take on new projects | set goals | cut new keys
     Keyhole – caution; Check the locks; stay safe

King – leadership
     Wear a suit | be patient | take on leadership role

Kite – good things are lost; job loss
     Find new work | mind your belongings | fly a kite

Lace – marriage and family
     Get married | have kids | count your blessings

Ladder – a leader and influencer helps you find fortune
Consult experts | ask for a raise | change bulbs

Lake – calm; mental rest
Do yoga | believe in yourself | go to a lake

Lamp – success in business; foolhardiness
Take on a new project | take a risk | redecorate

Lantern – a false sense of security
Be mindful of trusting others |
eat camp food

Light bulb – something will be revealed; an idea
Turn on the lights | write down your thoughts

Lighthouse – safety at sea; a fun cruise
Take a boat trip or cruise | eat seafood

Lightning – bad weather; death; loss
Check weather | wear a coat | celebrate a life

Litter/Trash – irresponsibility; laziness
Pick up your trash | declutter | take ownership

Lock – lack of success
Motivate yourself | keep working | buy a safe

Magnet – a crush; an affection for the wrong person
Be mindful of your heart | be wary of others

Magnifying Glass – watch for hyperbole; lies
    Someone might be dishonest with you | don't lie

Mail/Post – an obstacle blocks your way
    Push forward | set goals | check the mail

Mask – hidden intentions; lies
    Prep for criticism | follow clues | costume shop

Mermaid – shipwreck; trouble at sea
    Avoid boats | wear a lifejacket | vegan for a day

Meteor – sudden fortune
    Be open to receive good luck | guard your success

Mirror – take note of your hopes and dreams
    Look to other symbols for more information

Moon – fortune and recognition; astrology: Cancer
    Look at the moon | get a raise | celebrate wins

Mountain – powerful friends and enemies; ambition
    Go for a hike | chase small goals to attain big
    successes | show courage and strength

Music: Conductor/notes/etc – good luck for a musician
    If not musical, stay positive | encouraging news

Nail – labor; hard work
    fix broken items | be self-employed | work out

Necklace – a gift; if broken – a bond is shattered
> Give and receive gifts | broken necklace – beware

Needle – trickery
> Watch for wolves in sheep clothing | patch holes

Net – very hard work brings prosperous returns
> Watch news | take on new tasks | play basketball

Obelisk – remembering the deceased; praising deities
> Thank your deity | remember elders | send mail

Olympic rings – unity; travel
> Travel abroad | watch the Olympics | play a game

Package – worries; loss; doing what is expected
> Send a package | relax | become a delivery person

Pants – interacting with others
> Go on LinkedIn | buy new pants | lead your team
> **Underwear** – interacting with others in secret

Pail – activities you're not fond of
> Do hard chores | clean the eaves | dig

Palace – good fortune; someone does you a favor
> Request a favor | celebrate yourself and others

Parachute – safety; everything goes to plan
> Take careful steps | be satisfied with your work

People – usually a good omen; depends on event
>   Look to other symbols for more info on events

Pendulum – success in industry; reliability
>   Get into the swing of things | be trustworthy

Piano – advancement; making the most of a situation
>   Ask for a promotion | get a new job | learn piano

Pillar – enduring strength; permanence
>   You are in a good place | enjoy stability

Pitchfork – a feud
>   Prepare for a debate | visit a museum

Planets

>   Planets might be a message to combine astrology
>   with your Tea Leaf reading. Look at the main
>   astrological sign or house of the planets seen.
>   Do they feature in your chart, or someone else's?
>   See also: Moon (Cancer) or Sun (Leo)

>   Read your horoscope | stargaze | use a telescope

>   **Earth** – material gain; wealth accumulates; mother
>   nature
>   **Mercury** – thoughts; communication; difficult
>   changes; Gemini & Virgo
>   **Mars** – Maleness; fire; ruthlessness; war; Aries &
>   Scorpio (classical)
>   **Neptune** – subconscious mind; dreams and
>   fantasies; Pisces (new)

Jupiter – expansion; opening our minds;
Sagittarius & Pisces (classical)

Saturn – restriction; boundaries; difficult work;
Capricorn & Aquarius (classical)

Pluto – transformation; death and rebirth;
Scorpio (new)

Uranus – awakening; change; surprises;
Aquarius (new)

Venus – love; relationships; beauty; finances;
Taurus & Libra

Pope/Religious figure – tradition; business failure
Do not take advantage | start over | be good

Purse – theft
Watch your belongings | secure locks | buy a safe

Pyramid – fame; power; wealth
Believe in yourself | get a haircut | give back

Quarter – 1/4th; seasons; saving money
Save your money | accept gifts | open the mail

Queen – royalty; feminine power; strength
Be a mother | adopt a pet | buy land | make money

Quilt – connections; family
Reach out to family and friends | make a quilt

Racquet – defenses are down; psychological attacks
Find a support group | watch *Split* | play tennis

Raft – a need to listen to your intuition

    Meditate, what is your body and mind telling you?

Railway – warning

    Fix the car | fill up your tires | ride the train

Rainbow – fortune; good luck; wishes come true

    Make a wish | celebrate St Patty's | walk outside

    Rain – foreboding; introspection; end to drought

Rake – cleaning up; getting rid of the old

    Declutter | donate unused items | make space

Razor – disputes; disagreements; separation

    Break up | ask for a divorce | go to court

Ring – a business transaction

    Look to other symbols for more info on this deal

River – grief; trouble brewing

    Prepare for sad events | go on a hike | go fish

Road – smooth: steady path to goals; bumpy: obstacles

    Re-evaluate your goals | keep moving | road trip

Rocket – a joyful event right around the corner

    Throw a party | accept invitations | eat fruit

Rocking Chair – a successful idea relating to children

    Invent a game or toy | babysit | eat spaghetti

Rocks – a caution about avoiding trouble

      Be wary of dangerous paths | collect pretty rocks

Rolling pin – a smooth path ahead

      Bake | go on a hike | try something new

Running, humans– an emergency; urgent messages

      Be wary of rushing | work diligently | plan ahead

      Running shoes – speedy work turns out well

Saddle – freedom after attaining goals

      set goals | horseback riding | watch Secretariat

Sailboat – a change for the better

      Embrace new things | move | go sailing

Satellite – broadband communications

      Watch *Social Network* | do social media | stargaze

Saw – someone interferes with an important project

      Say no | do carpentry | distrust your coworkers

Scaffolding – jumping into projects too quickly

      Slow down | follow the plan | watch *The Money Pit*

Scales – lawsuit

      Call your lawyer | become a lawyer | measure food

Scarecrow – stay out of other peoples' business

      Mind your own business | visit a farmer's market

Scissors – disagreements with partners; business trouble

    Make plans | don't fight | stick to business

Scoop – the tables turn and cause confusion

    Watch out | eat ice cream | take a chance | study

Screw – perseverance gets you to your goal
Set goals | do creative projects | eat
granola

Scythe – aggression; supernatural beings

    Join an anger management class | go ghost hunting

Seesaw – comparing yourself to others

    Stop comparing yourself to others | don't judge

Shell/Conch – listen to your emotions; feel something

    Go to the beach | journal your emotions

Ship – a visitor or news from abroad; travel

    Take a cruise | read the mail | eat seafood

Shirt – lucky events

    Accept invitations | buy a new shirt | say yes

Shovel or Trowel – good weather conditions

    Dig weeds | wear light clothing | drink a smoothie

Slippers – repetitive behaviors; showing off

    Avoid bragging | watch a movie | eat popcorn

Snowflakes – a child approaches; a new baby; February
Play in snow | babysit | work with kids | play

Soap – trouble at work
Quit your job | take a long shower | make soap

Socks – clean: trustworthiness; dirty: bad reputation
Do laundry | buy a pair of socks | donate socks

Sofa – nightmares; a health emergency
Rest | see your doctor | record your dreams

Staple – organization
clean your house | sort closets | do paperwork

Steps – a coworker quits and the work is added to yours
Demand assistance | fix the creaky staircase

Stones – small worries
Meditate | make a list of to-dos | do chores

Submarine – a secret is disclosed
Watch the news | listen to others | gossip | go
scuba diving

Suitcase – arrivals and departures
Visit the airport | travel | check your suitcase

Sun – happiness & discovery; attraction; astrology: Leo
Throw a party | drink wine | cater an event

Sundial – take note of how you spend your time
>   Look to other symbols for info on things to do

Swimming – overcoming your fears
>   Swim | practice immersion therapy | greet spiders
>   **Swimsuit** – taking back your power

Sword – danger; death; gossip
>   Be wary of others | don't answer the door

Tambourine – a fun event with friends; singing
>   Accept invitations | go camping | throw a party

Teddy bear – childhood
>   Read books to children | stop languishing

Telephone – forgetfulness
>   Write it down | seek lost items | answer calls

Telescope – trouble with your vision
>   go to eye doctor | wear your glasses | read

Tennis – social events
>   Play tennis | call a friend | go to an event

Tent – travel
>   Travel | go camping | eat trail mix

Thimble – a spinster; changes at home
>   Learn to knit | create something | break up

Tomb – failure

      Re-evaluate your actions | visit a gravesite

Tower – a promotion

      Get promoted | choose hard work | be self-employed

Toys – enjoying time with children

      Play | become a teacher | eat macaroni & cheese

Train – travel; someone arrives

      Answer the door | invite over a friend | vacation

Trumpet – entertainment; a group of fans

      See a movie | see a concert | watch a musical

Tunnel – a bad decision is made

      Choose wisely | don't take chances | don't travel

Ukelele – Hawaiian culture and history

      Visit Hawaii | play music | embrace your heritage

Umbrella – open: bad weather; closed: bad luck

      Be careful | wear a jacket | clean the gutters

University – academia; understanding; knowledge

      Follow tradition | go to school | be a professor

Urn – illness; death

      Attend a funeral | cremate the dead | eat cheese

Van – a successful experiment

    Try something new | try chemistry | drive a van

Vase – Good health

    Visit the doctor | eat healthy | take vitamins

Vault – a promotion; held in high esteem

    Accept a promotion | visit the bank | volunteer

Villa – inner demons

    Listen to your subconscious | travel to Europe

Violin – for a musician: good luck; entertainment

    Write a song | see a movie | listen to classics

Volcano– a rash; blemishes; mental health problems

    Calm down | see a doctor | wash your face

    Eruption – a violent outburst

Wagon – journey to a better life

    Take a trip | relocate for work | visit family

Wall – obstacles

    Plant ivy | watch your step | eat different foods

Wand – psychic abilities

    Become a fortune teller | consult tarot cards

Weathervane – indecision; constantly questioning

    Choose a new direction | watch Hamlet | repaint

Wheel – the wheel of fortune; wealth
Gamble | clean the den | eat tangerines

Windmill – hope
Go berry picking | meditate | walk a dog

Window – people see you as good (open) or bad (closed)
Clean the windows | go outside | open a window

Wings – changes for the better; free of restrictions
Push through challenges | go birdwatching

Witch – your psychic ability worries friends
Read the tarot and runes | trust your intuition

Wizard – justice; law
Prepare for court | watch Law & Order | dress up

X-Ray – poor health; financial problems
Visit the doctor | check accounts |
pay bills

Xylophone – harmony in specific areas of your life
Play a xylophone | give gifts to children

Yacht – good fortune
Go sailing | take a trip | buy a yacht

You – negative interpretations of yourself
List your best traits, inside & out | be yourself

Yo-Yo – an incompetent person; fluctuating situations
  Stay steady | ride the wave | play yo-yo

Zombie – death; enemies (D&D)
  Play a role-playing game | watch a Zombie movie

Zipper – keeping closed-mouthed
  Zip your lips | avoid gossip | fix your zipper

Zoo – people do not give you enough credit; being caged
  Cull social media contacts | go to the zoo

Notes, doodles, or other objects you see:

Fig. 6

My middle kid, David, sees Saturn exploding. The rings stretch from left to right, and the planet bursts in the center. He sees nothing else.

Saturn represents boundaries and a need for hard work which, as a junior in University, he knows he must focus on. In his natal astrology chart, Saturn is in his 12th house, which can sometimes mean it's hard to get recognition in one's field. David's field is acting and music, so he will have to "burst" pretty hard through that planet position to be seen.

Explosions indicate hard truths that can upset friends. David is a very honest guy, so he has to be careful with being *too* honest and hurting people's feelings. All true, he admits.

Letters and Numbers

Letters might be initials, memos, or something that you need to spell out for yourself. You can use numbers to represent dates, amounts, addresses, times, whatever numbers you need.

The following include some other possible interpretations for specific letters and numbers, taken from various sources including Numerology, astrology, and ancient wisdom.

A – the start of something new

　　Take a chance | clean high shelves | first place

B – house; body; birth; sharing of ideas

　　Write down your goals | invent | "be/bee"

C – luck; messages from spirit; 100

　　Trust your intuition | take a chance | "see"

D – ten days; ten years; completion; music; 500

　　Finish a project | write a song | drive

E – Mother Earth; intuition

　　Garden | take care of the planet | fill tank "E"

F – truth; the end of a journey

　　Finish your projects | listen to others | "F***"

G – buildings; architecture; sacred geometry

　　Design or build something | question | "gee"

H – a visionary; the four winds of heaven; safety

　　Secure locks | check the weather | Hydrogen

I – fishing; the spine; intuition; 1

　　Trust your gut | take care of the self – "I"

J – the hands; self-determination; potential

　　Learn ASL | study new things | joking

K – an open palm; teamwork; collaboration

      Collaborate | help others | Kilobyte | "OK"

L – the legs; balance; 50

      Go for a walk | stretch | "Lose"

M – the world; chasing one's dreams; 1000

      Write down your goals | create | Mega | Million

N – clever people; strong wills

      Be confident | talk to others | "No"

O – new opportunities; sharing

      Say yes | meet people | circle of friends | "Oh!"

P – knowledge; insight; talent; energy

      Practice skills | exercise | text friends | pee

Q – challenges; uncooperative people

      Reply to emails | work independently | Queer | "?"

R – potential; offering of service

      Perform a service | join a nonprofit | reverse direction

S – the self; independence

      Take care of your body | be self-employed | small

T – coexistence; a house; protection

      Move in with someone | countdown | drink tea

U – give and take; collection

    Use | give/receive gifts | collect items | "You"

V – one door closes, another opens; 5

    Look for other opportunities | "very" | "versus"

W – adaptation

    Prepare for change | "Win"

X – home; high ideals; 10

    Make plans | stay in | treasure hunt | "kiss"

Y – curiosity; solving problems

    Ask questions | do a puzzle | "Why?"

Z – endings; peace and organization

    Celebrate successes | finish a project | numbers

0 – nothingness

    Do nothing | clear your head | go for a walk

1 – courage; beginnings

    Start something new | get a new job | place 1st

2 – femininity; partnership; refinement

    Make a decision | go on a date | learn to juggle |
    balance the budget

3 – creativity; imagination

    Look to the future | follow your dreams | party

4 – balance; patience

> Build a table | watch Star Trek | read *1984*

5 – curiosity; change; mobility

> Relocate | move the furniture | watch The Martian

6 – harmony; family

> Celebrate with family | read *Six of Crows*

7 – exploration; self-analysis

> Visit a career coach | read a self-help manual

8 – wisdom; confidence; personality

> Travel | consult an eight ball | Read

9 – communication; diversity

> Watch *Arrival* | join a protest | join a cause

11, 22, or 33 – in numerology these are special numbers
meaning increased energy, power, enlightenment

Other characters:

+ - addition

− - subtraction

÷ - division

æ – the Rune Ansuz; God; a special message

> Look to other symbols to infer the message
> also consider Rune shapes as letters, too. Read
> *Applied Runes*[4] for more information.

---

[4] Applied Runes is available here https://amzn.to/3QhOEVC

Notes, doodles, or other words you see:

Fig. 7

In a mid-day cup I see a giant S, a demon
(distress), a bee (success through own
skills), and a bunch of dashes (work). I
think the S stand for my sister, Sue. For
an article I'm writing, I have to
interview her about some of her job
annoyances. Sue is the bee (S, successful)
dealing with demons (distress) at her
dashes (work)!

Miscellaneous Symbols

Certain shapes may hold significant meaning for you, so always be sure to trust your own personal intuition when reading the tea leaves.

∩ **Arch** – desired items will come to fruition; hope

Travel | get married | create a wishlist | paint

Chain – a series of connected events; responsibility

Follow the chain | take ownership | attachment

Circles – unexpected gifts; the circle of life

Say yes | show gratitude | pay it forward | ring

Crescent – introspection; rest

See a psychic | meditate | trust your intuition

Column – a need to build something

Take direction | architect a house or project

Comma – making progress; taking a break

Rest | bookmark your pages | stop working today

† **Cross** – misfortune and grief

Attend a funeral | seek help | go to church

Cube/Sphere/Pyramid – realization of goals

Make plans and stick to them | protect yourself

Curve – voice; sounds

Speak | practice accents | write a song

Dashes – a short trip; keeping busy; work

Work hard | leave the house |
go shopping

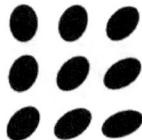

Dots - representative of money; look to other symbols to figure out where money is coming and going

Helix/corkscrew - your talents sent from the divine; Keep practicing | prepare for challenges

∞ **Infinity** - love; connection; a tie that binds
Start dating | get married | commit | do math

Line, forked - a decision has to be made
See if the forks point to further symbols

Lines - journey; wavy lines mean difficult travel
Direction of lines tell where the journey leads

♂ **Man** - man; action; mars

Ask a man for help | smash the patriarchy

(((**Motion lines** - movement; echoes
Sing; go hiking | look to other symbols

Ω **Omega** - greatness; arrogance
Remain kind | give back | don't hold back

Oval - the reproductive system
Adopt kittens | get birth control | visit a doctor

Pentagon - control; authority; tough times ahead
You will get through this | stick to the plan

Question Mark - doubts; indecision

Ask questions | answer others | make a choice

Semicircle - half conscious and half unconscious

Trust your gut | finish a project | change

Spiral - success in industry

Launch a business | work in manufacturing | build

Squares - peace and comfort

Relax | protect your surroundings | box items up

Star - good luck; if surrounded by dots: new money

Take a chance | start a new business | stargazing

Σ Sum - bringing together; a net

Do the math | work with others | manifest

Triangle - a legacy; fortune

Look to other symbols for where the fortune comes from | write your will

Ψ Trident - choices; capture; the sea

Take a cruise | read | invoke Neptune | eat fish

Waves - water; purification; travel

Travel on water | visit the beach | ride the wave

♀ Woman - a woman; romance; love; Venus

Ask a woman for advice | call mom | make money

Zeppelin – career takes off; standing up for yourself
     Be confident | read fantasy novels | study history

ZigZag – the path of your life; confidence in your work
     do not question yourself | keep going this way

Notes, doodles, or other symbols you see:

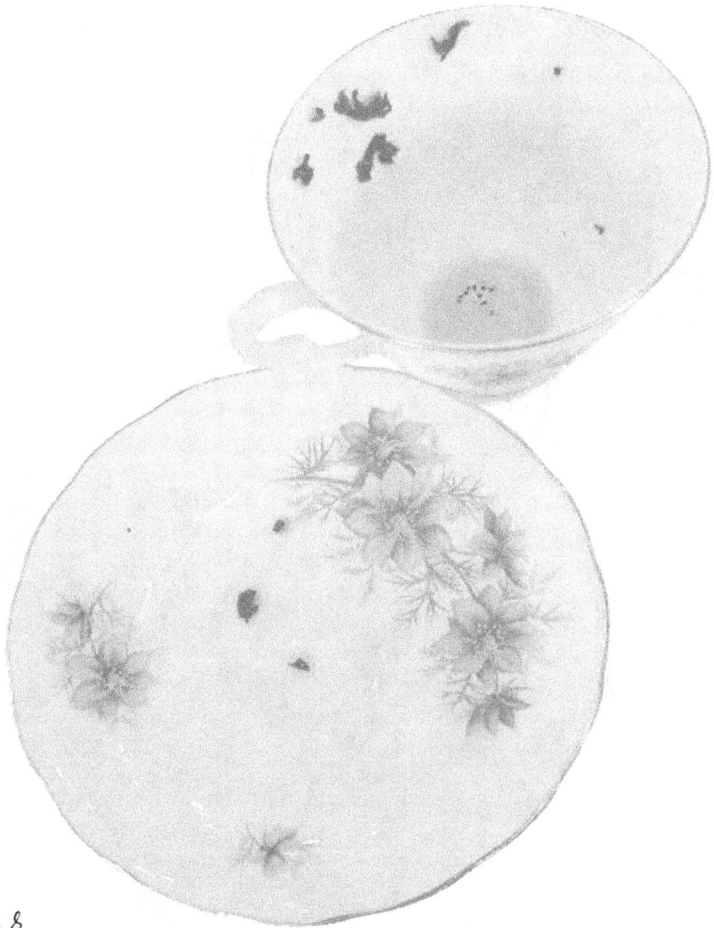

Fig. 8

I did a past, present, future reading for myself.
In my past I see a bat (recent illness), a bird of
paradise flower (it ended quickly,) a bee about to
land on it (hard work,) and a dove (entrepreneurial
success.) I'm working hard on this tea leaves
manual, so hopefully success comes. Below the
flower is an arch (love, perhaps a wedding? No
rush, kids!) At the very bottom, or far future, is
an arrow of dots (money woes - oh no!)

If I count the saucer as things I need more of,
there is a frog (a new job - true) and some darts
(struggle - boo! But sure, I'm up for a challenge.)

Notes, doodles, or other symbols you see:

Other Drinks

Why stop at tea?
I already told you why – tea trees have been around for
thousands of years, and will be around for thousands of
years more, and these other plants haven't and won't.

However, tea isn't everyone's cup of tea (ha!) and there
could be plenty of random things at the bottom of your
cup, so here are some other ideas for drinks!

Coffee

I wasn't about to let a drink divination manual go by without mentioning my favorite caffeinated beverage!

In the 18th century, Italians invented a divination method, similar to Tasseography, out of coffee grounds (because of course they did! They're experts at coffee.)

Funnily enough, those original Italian diviners believed the symbols at the bottom of coffee cups were messages from Demons, so they're almost always bad. I don't know why they would do this, nor why anyone would want to have a reading *knowing* the prophecies they're getting are negative, but who knows why people do what they do?

So, with coffee you can use the same symbols as in tasseography. Some messages are good, most are bad, all of it is fun!

Traditionally, coffee diviners used Turkish coffee, or any coffee that leaves grinds at the bottom of the cup after drinking most of the liquid. You can swirl these around and then flip the cup over into a saucer, or leave the cup to let the sediment dry before reading.

One thing to remember is that - whereas tea trees live for thousands of years and have thus seen the beginnings and endings of human history - coffee plants only live max 100 years and are usually only productive in their early age. In this regard a tea leaf reading is more trustworthy, but coffee is just fun. Don't expect your grounds to "see" anything more than a few years in the past or future, however.

Fruit Punch

Not the fake, already prepared stuff you buy in the
juice aisle - I mean fruit punch that you've made
yourself, possibly on a hot, sunny day, that you're
sharing with friends. Prepare a punchbowl filled with
your favorite chopped fruits, juices, maybe a spritzer
or two, and some ice. Grab a glass and toast to a lovely
sunset. When the ice has melted and the glass is empty,
see which fruity shapes remain at the bottom of your
cup.

Herbal Tea

As mentioned in chapter one, herbal tea is not real tea,
but you can still use it if you're out of the real
thing, or if you're unable to drink natural tea for
whatever reason. Peppermint trees can live from 40 to
150 years, so there is still a bit of wisdom in a hot
cup of peppermint, even if it isn't real tea.

Wine Sediments

Drink your favorite glass of red wine (red is easier to
see than white, however white wine does leave sediment
as well) and see what lies beneath. The best wines for
this are typically vintages that are over ten years old.
The older a wine is, the more likely it is to have
sediment - not to mention being better able to see your
future than those newfangled wines.

The older the wine, the wiser the wine!

Sediment is a healthy, organic byproduct of the
fermentation process, so don't be afraid to drink it or
see tons of it in your glass.

Whatever

I don't know what else leaves drink remains. Beer? Boba?
Kombucha? Badly mixed Kool Aid? If you see a symbol at
the bottom of a random drink, dive in! Maybe the
universe is trying to tell you something.

More from Applied Divination

Applied Tarot by Emily Paper
Applied Tarot Reversed by Emily Paper
Applied Runes by Emily Paper

Psychic Word Puzzles by Applied Divination
Divination Journal by Applied Divination

Faye's Fortune by Emmy Tidning
Charlie's Chill by Emmy Tidning

Coming soon:
Sloane's Solitude by Emmy Tidning

Image Credits

Fig. 3 photographed by Margaret P.
All images created or edited with permission by Emily
Paper.

About the Author

Emily Paper is a divination and Feng Shui specialist
working on a master's degree in Smashing the Patriarchy
(it's a thing) and a doctorate in pantheism.

With over 35 years of random fortune telling experience,
it took losing a set of car keys to inspire her to write
the first book in this series, *Applied Tarot*.

Emily lives with her husband and pets in Washington
State. She can be found wandering around various social
medias, and at www.emilypaper.com

Acknowledgements

Thanks to everyone who bought or browsed my first three
divination manuals, *Applied Tarot, Applied Tarot
Reversed,* and *Applied Runes.*

This book is dedicated to my three university-going
children, for whom I need to pay tuition this year.
That's a lotta tea.

Applied Spells

A Practical Guide to Manifesting Dreams, Blessing Friends, and ~~Cursing Enemies~~ Other Magik

Killer of indoor plants? Got a black thumb?

Try de-chlorinating your tap water by leaving it out on the counter for 24 hours,
And set it outside on a full moon to collect metaphysical energy!
Your snake plant will bless you with abundance and prosperity! Or, at the very least, it should stay alive.

Hint:
Put me
in your
Wealth or
Fame gua!

Follow emilypaper.com for more information!

www.ingramcontent.com/pod-product-compliance
Lightning Source LLC
LaVergne TN
LVHW021402080426
835508LV00020B/2406